THE LETTERS OF GRACCHUS ON THE EAST INDIA QUESTION

First published 1813
This edition published by Lector House in 2023

ISBN: 978-93-5800-755-8

Lector House LLP
Registered Office: H. No. 96, Block C, Tomar Colony,
Burari, Delhi – 110084, India
info@lectorhouse.com
www.lectorhouse.com

THE LETTERS OF GRACCHUS ON THE EAST INDIA QUESTION

WILLIAM AUGUSTUS MILES

2023

LECTOR HOUSE LLP

THE LETTERS GRACCHUS ON THE EAST INDIA QUESTION.

ADVERTISEMENT.

The following Letters appeared in the MORNING POST, at the dates which are annexed to them. The impartial Reader will find in them a strong determination, to uphold the public rights of the Country, with respect to the India Trade; but he will not discover any evidence of a desire to lower the just, and well-earned honours, of THE EAST INDIA COMPANY, nor any symptom of a disposition hostile to their fair pretensions.

CONTENTS

LETTERS OF GRACCHUS.

LETTER I.

GENERAL VIEW OF THE EAST INDIA QUESTION.

Tuesday, January 12, 1813.

The crisis, at which the affairs of the East India Company are now arrived, is one which involves the most important interests of the British Empire. It would be unnecessary to prove a proposition which is so universally acknowledged and felt. It has happened however, that, in our approaches towards this crisis, the Public understanding has been but little addressed upon the subject; so that the appeal which is now suddenly made to their passions and imaginations, finds them unprepared with that knowledge of the true circumstances of the case, which can alone enable them to govern those passions, and control those imaginations. Let us then endeavour to recover the time which has been lost, by taking a deliberate view of the circumstances which produce this crisis.

The crisis, is the proximity of the term which may conclude the East India Company's rights, to the exclusive trade with India and China, and to the powers of government now exercised by them over the Indian Empire.

The rights of the East India Company are two-fold; and have long been distinguished as, their *permanent* rights, and their *temporary* rights. Those rights are derived to them from distinct Charters, granted to them at different times by Parliament. By the former, they were created a *perpetual* Corporate Society of Merchants, trading to India[1]. By the latter, they obtained, for a *limited period of time,* the exclusive right of trading with India and China, and of executing the powers of government over those parts of the Indian territory, which were acquired either by conquest or by negotiation. The Charter conveying the latter limited rights, is that which will expire in the course of the ensuing year 1814; on the expiration of which, the exclusive trade to the East will be again open to the British population at large, and the powers of the India Government will lapse in course to the Supreme Government of the British Empire, to be provided for as Parliament in its wisdom may judge it advisable to determine.

The renewal of an *expired* privilege cannot be pursued upon a ground of *right.* The exclusive Charter of the Company is *a patent,* and their patent, like every other patent, is limited as to *its duration*. But though the patentee cannot allege a ground

[1] The *rights and pretensions* of the Company are fully considered in the Tenth Letter.

of right for the renewal of his patent, he may show such strong pretensions, such good claims in equity, such weighty reasons of expediency for its renewal, as may ensure its attainment. Such are the claims and the pretensions of the East India Company to a renewal of their Charter; and as such they have been promptly and cheerfully received, both by the Government and the country at large.

But the progress of society, during a long course of years, is of a nature to produce a considerable alteration in the general state of things; the state of things must, therefore, naturally be called into consideration, upon the expiration of the term of years which determines the exclusive Charter of the East India Company; in order to inquire, whether that Charter should be renewed precisely in the same terms, and with the same conditions, as before; or whether the actual state of public affairs demands, that some alteration, some modification, of terms and conditions, should be introduced into the Charter or System which is to succeed.

The arduous task of this investigation must necessarily fall upon those persons, who chance to be in the Administration of the Country, at the latest period to which the arrangements for the renewal of the Charter can be protracted; and it is hardly possible to imagine a more difficult and perplexing position, for any Administration. Those persons, if they have any regard for the duties which they owe to the Public, will consider themselves as standing *between two interests*; the interest of those who are about to lose an exclusive right, and the interest of those who are about to acquire an open and a common one. They will be disposed to listen, patiently and impartially, to the pretensions of both parties; of those who pray for the renewal of an exclusive privilege, and of those who pray that they may not be again wholly excluded from the right which has reverted. And although they may amply allow the preference which is due to the former petitioners, yet they will endeavour to ascertain, whether the latter may not, with safety to the public interest, receive some enlargement of the benefits, which the opportunity opens to them, and from which they have been so long excluded.

While they thus look alternately to each of these interests, and are engaged in striving to establish a reconciliation between the two, it will be neither equitable nor liberal for one of the interested parties to throw out a doubt to the Public, whether they do this "from a consciousness of strength, and a desire of increasing their own power and influence, or from a sense of weakness and a wish to strengthen themselves by the adoption of popular measures[2]." And the author of the doubt may find himself at length obliged to determine it, by an awkward confession, that Ministers do not do it "with any view of augmenting their own patronage and power[3]."

It is thus that the Ministers of the Crown have conducted themselves, in the embarrassing crisis into which they have fallen. Fully sensible of the just and honourable pretensions which the East India Company have established in the course of their long, important, and distinguished career, they have consented to recommend to Parliament, *to leave the whole system of Indian Government and Revenue to the Company,* under the provisions of the Act of 1793; together with *the exclusive trade*

[2] Considerations on the Danger of laying open the Trade with India and China, p. 13.
[3] Ibid. p. 18.

to China, as they have hitherto possessed them; but, at the same time, considering the present state of the world, and its calamitous effects upon the commercial interest in general, they are of opinion, that some participation in the Indian trade, thus reverting, might possibly be conceded, under due regulations, to British merchants not belonging to the East India Company; which would not impair the interests either of the Public or of the Company.

In this moderate opinion, they are fully justified, by the consent of the Company, to admit the Merchants of the out-ports to a share in the Indian trade. And thus far, all is amicable. But the out-port Merchants having represented to Government, that the condition, hitherto annexed to a Licensed Import Trade,—of bringing back their Indian Cargoes to the port of London, and of disposing of them solely in the Company's sales, in Leadenhall Street,—would defeat the object of the concession; and that the delay, embarrassment, and perplexity, which such an arrangement would create, would destroy the simple plan of their venture; and having therefore desired, that they might be empowered to return with their cargoes to the ports from whence they originally sailed, and to which all their interests are confined; Government, being convinced of the justice of the representation, have proposed that the Import Trade may be yielded to the Out-ports, *under proper regulations*, as well as the Export Trade. To this demand the Court of Directors peremptorily refuse their consent; and upon this *only point* the parties are now at issue. This question alone, retards the final arrangements for the renewal of their Charter.

Yet it is this point, which one of the parties interested affirms, to be "a question of the last importance to the safety of the British Empire in India, and of the British Constitution at home;" and therefore undertakes to resist it, with all the determination which the importance of so great a stake would naturally inspire. But, when we compare the real measure in question with the menacing character which is thus attempted to be attached to it, we at once perceive something so extravagantly hyperbolical, something so disproportionate, that it at once fixes the judgment; and forces upon it a suspicion, that there is more of policy and design, than of truth and sincerity in the assertion. That objections to the measure might arise, capable of distinct statement and exposition, is a thing conceivable; and, these being stated, it would be a subject for consideration, how far they were removable. But to assert, in a round period, that the safety of the empire in Europe and Asia is fundamentally affected in the requisition, that a ship proceeding from Liverpool or Bristol to India, might return from India to Liverpool or Bristol, instead of to the Port of London, is calculated rather to shake, than to establish, confidence in those who make the assertion. Yet this is the question which the country is now called upon to consider, as one tending to convulse the British Constitution. Surely, if the foundations of the empire in both hemispheres have nothing more to threaten them, than whether the out-port shipping shall carry their cargoes home to their respective ports, or repair to the dock-yards in the port of London, the most timid politician may dismiss his alarms and resume his confidence. When the East India Company, by conceding a regulated Export Trade, have at once demonstrated the absurdity of all the predictions which foretold, in that Trade, the overthrow of the

Indian Empire; we may confidently believe, that the Import Trade will prove as little destructive, and that its danger will be altogether as chimerical as the former.

Whether the Court of Directors endeavour to fix that menacing character upon the proposed Import Trade, as a bar against any further requisition, is a question which will naturally occur to any dispassionate person, who is not immediately and personally interested in the conditions of the Charter; and he will be strongly inclined to the affirmative in that question, when he finds, that the reason which they have alleged for their resistance, is their apprehension of the increased activity which the practice of smuggling would acquire, from the free return of the out-port ships from India to their respective ports. It is not a little extraordinary, that they should so strenuously urge this argument against those persons, who, while they propose the measure, are themselves responsible for the good management and protection of the revenue; and who must therefore be supposed to feel the necessity of providing means and regulations, adapted to the measure which they propose. The Ministers of the Crown have not failed to inform the Court of Directors, that, in consequence of the communications which they have had with the Commissioners of the Customs and Excise upon the subject, they find that the Directors have greatly over-rated the danger which they profess to entertain; and they acquaint them, that new regulations will be provided to meet the new occasion; and that the out-port ships and cargoes will be subject to forfeiture upon the discovery of any illicit articles on board. Yet the Court of Directors still persist in declaring, that the hazard of *smuggling* is *the reason* why they will not grant to the out-ports an import trade; and this, through a fear of compromising "the safety of the British Empire in India, and the British Constitution at home."

A calm and temperate observer, who scrupulously weighs the force and merits of this reasoning, will naturally be forced into so much scepticism as to doubt, whether there may not be some *other reasons*, besides the safety of the Empire, which may induce the East India Company to stand so firm for the condition of bringing all the import Indian trade *into the Port of London*? Whether there may not be some reasons, of a *narrower* sphere than those of the interests of the Empire? In searching for such reasons, it will occur to him, that the Port of London is the seat of the Company's immediate and separate interests; and he will shrewdly suspect, that those interests are the *real*, while those of the Empire are made the *ostensible*, motive for so vigorous a resistance. When he reflects, *that it is proposed to leave the Company in the undisturbed possession of all the power of Government over the Indian Empire, which they have hitherto enjoyed; that they are to remain possessed, as heretofore, of the exclusive trade to China, from whence four-fifths of their commercial profit is derived*; that they themselves have virtually admitted the falsity of the theoretical mischiefs, foretold as the certain results of an out-port trade, by having agreed to concede that trade, to the extent required by Government; that they equally allow, an import trade for the merchants of the out-ports; but make their resistance upon the single point, that the import trade should be all brought together into their own warehouses, and should be disposed of in their own sales in Leadenhall Street: when he combines all these considerations, he will think that he plainly discovers, that the interests of the Empire at large are not quite so much involved in the question as they proclaim; and that, if any interests are more pressingly calculated than others, it must be their own, and not the Public's. If their interests are to be affected by the measure, let them fairly state it, and show the extent; but let them not endeavour to defend them covertly, under an artful and factious allegation of *the ruin of the British Constitution*. And if they really do apprehend that the Constitution would be endangered, let them not hazard such consequences by their own proceedings. Let them not come forward as advocates for the preservation of the Empire, if their rhetoric is to sink into a threat, of *"shutting up the great shop of the India House."*

It may be well to call to the recollection of the East India Company, that they owe their present state to an assertion of those very rights to open trade which have now been brought forward; for, when the first, or London East India Company had experienced certain disappointments and failures, various adventurers came forward with claims similar to those which have been alleged by the merchants of the present day, and obtained an incorporation, to the prejudice of the old Company; and although the old, or London East India Company, afterwards effected an union with the new, or English East India Company, and with them gave origin to the present Company, yet the UNITED EAST INDIA COMPANY should not forget, how much the activity of the Indian trade was stimulated by the assertion of the rights of their predecessors, *to participate in the trade which had been granted exclusively to a former Company.*

GRACCHUS.

LETTER II.

Wednesday, January 13, 1813.

It is a distinguishing character appertaining to Britons, to express forcibly their feelings, whenever they think they discover any disposition to encroach upon their rights. It is not therefore to be wondered at, that the communication of the papers, on the subject of the East India Company's Charter, which was made by the Directors to the Proprietors, on the 5th instant, should have produced the effect which was then manifested; of an almost unanimous disposition, to support the Directors in their resistance of a measure, which, at the time, was regarded as an invasion, on the part of the Government, of the established rights of the East India Company.

But now that the momentary ebullition of that spirit has had time to subside, and to give place to cool and sober reflection, it may not be unacceptable to the Proprietors at large to look calmly and attentively into the subject; and to examine its bearings on their own substantial interests.

It must be manifest to every man, who will only refer to the accounts which have been published in the Reports of the Select Committee of the House of Commons, that, from the magnitude of the Company's debt, it would be impossible to calculate the time at which the Proprietors could contemplate any augmentation of their present dividends of 10½ per cent.; even though the Charter, instead of being within one year of its expiration, had an extended period of twenty years to operate.

It is equally manifest, from the correspondence of the Court of Directors with Government, that, in agreeing to the proposition of opening the Export Trade to the out-ports of the United Kingdom, they were free from any apprehension, that the continuance of the present dividend could be endangered by their conceding that point. And, therefore, although the Proprietors were precluded from entertaining any reasonable expectation of *an increase* to their dividends, they were perfectly warranted to consider the continuance of that which they now receive, as free from any hazard, in consequence of the extension proposed to be granted to the Export Trade.

Whether they may remain in the same confidence, under *all* existing circumstances, is a question which the Proprietors are now earnestly solicited to examine. The point at issue (if I may apply that expression to a case, in which the Company are upon the disadvantageous ground of petitioning for the renewal of a privilege, now about to expire) is, whether the ships which shall be permitted to clear out from the out-ports of the United Kingdom, ought to be allowed to return to any given description of those ports, or whether they should all be compelled to enter at the Port of London? And upon *this point* is made to hinge a question, which may affect (not the *British Empire and Constitution*, but) the main interest of the Proprietors, namely, *their dividends*. For no man can be so inconsiderately sanguine as to suppose, that the Company, under the present pressure of their pecuniary embarrassments, (whatever may have been the causes from whence they have arisen;) embarrassments proceeding from a debt, in India and in England, of *more than forty-two millions*; nearly four millions of which are in accepted bills on England, which will shortly become due, and for the payment of which there are not funds at the India House; no man can be so inconsiderately sanguine as to suppose, that the dividend may not become a little precarious, under such circumstances. It must be evident to the most superficial observer, that the credit of the Company with the Public can only be sustained by the prompt and liberal aid of Parliament; and it will hardly be maintained, that it is a *propitious* mode of soliciting that aid, to connect with the solicitation an avowed determination to oppose a measure, which Government represent it to be their duty to recommend to Parliament, for the general benefit of the community; a measure, founded on, and growing out of, the principle of the Charter of 1793, which first opened the private trade between India and this country; the provisions respecting which trade have been progressively extended at subsequent periods, and of which trade the Public will now call for a further enlargement and participation, as a just and necessary qualification to the proposed renewal of the Company's Charter.

The City of London, indeed, is *now* an exception, and apparently a very weighty one, to this general call; but it will lose much of that weight with the Public, and must fall into the scale of an interested party, when it is recollected, that so long as the question between the Company and the Public was, whether the commerce with India should remain a strict monopoly, or whether a participation in it should be granted to individuals, under the restriction of importing to London the commercial interest of the metropolis was powerfully incited against the Company; and that, to that great commercial interest, supported by the weight of Mr. Dundas's opinion, and to the more enlarged view which Lord Wellesley took of the subject, the extension that has hitherto been given to the private trade with India is to be attributed. The experience of twelve years has now proved, that both India and the parent state have greatly benefited by that extension; and it has followed, as a necessary consequence of that experience, that the active and intelligent merchants of the other large ports of the United Kingdom, have urged their fair pretensions, to be admitted to a share in the profits of that widely diffused trade; by sending their merchandise from their own ports, and by receiving the returning cargoes into their own warehouses, in those ports.

A reference to the printed papers (as has already been signified) will show, that the Court of Directors were prevailed upon to concede *the first* of those points, but that they have been immoveable with respect to *the second*; although their own commercial knowledge must have made it evident to them, that the concession of the first, that is, *a free export*, would be nugatory, unless supported by the benefit arising from the *freedom of import*; which is not only in the proportion of four to one in amount to the export, but is requisite to give that unity to the concern, without which great commercial establishments cannot be kept up.

Such is the state of the question, or, as it has been called, by some strange perversion of ideas, the *negotiation*, between the Company, as applicants for a renewal of their Charter which is about to expire, and the Government, through whose aid it is to be solicited, or at least, without whose concurrence it is certainly very questionable, whether they would be able to obtain it. These are the circumstances, under which the affairs of the East India Company must necessarily, and speedily, be brought forward, for the consideration of Parliament. Can it, then, be considered an exaggerated view of the hazards of such a situation, to suppose, that some guardian of the public purse may deem it requisite to inquire, whether the application for pecuniary aid from Parliament ought not to be preceded by a substantial proof, not of concession, for they have in fact nothing to concede, but of something like accommodation on the part of the Proprietors? And in that event, might it not be questioned, whether, since the dividend of 10 per cent. was sanctioned upon an assumption, that the revenue of the Company yielded a *surplus* of upwards of a million; now, when instead of a surplus, a *deficit* is admitted to exist, the dividend ought not to be reduced, not merely to the standard from which it had been raised under the supposed prosperous state of the Company's affairs, but to a standard to be regulated by the amount of the ascertained profits upon their own trade, under whatever circumstances it may hereafter be conducted?

It is not meant to insinuate, that any condition of the kind alluded to is likely to be imposed, in granting the relief so pressingly required by the present exigencies of the Company; but if a necessity for the winding up of their affairs, as an exclusive Company, should arrive, and if their own resources, with the profits they may derive from their commerce as a Corporate Body, should not be adequate to the payment of a dividend of 10½ per cent.; could it reasonably be expected, that Parliament would, in *all future times*, extend its liberality towards the Proprietors of India stock, to the extent of *securing to them* a continuance of their present dividend?

It is to be feared, that those who may have calculated upon such a result, have taken a false measure of their *prospective situation*; and it is on account of this apprehension, that it appears highly important to call the attention of the Proprietors to the care of their own substantial interest in the dividend; an interest, which to them is, and must be paramount.

GRACCHUS.

LETTER III.

Thursday, January 14, 1813.

It is at all times an object equally interesting and instructive, to trace the origin of laws and institutions, and to follow them in the progress of their operation; but this inquiry becomes more powerfully attractive, when the pursuit is stimulated by an anxiety to defend a supposed right, or to acquire an extension of advantages which are already possessed.

Such an investigation appearing to be a necessary sequel of the subject treated of in a former communication, let us now take a succinct view of those provisions of the Act of 1793, by which the East India Company, upon the last renewal of their Charter for a fixed time, were called upon to relax from the exclusive restrictions of the monopoly which they had so long enjoyed. Taking that Act as the source and origin from whence the present India Question arises, let us briefly follow the subject in its progress, down to the propositions that are now before the Public.

It is necessary to premise, that the Company had, from an early period of their commerce, granted as a favour and indulgence to the Captains and Officers of their ships, permission to fill a regular portion of tonnage with certain prescribed articles, upon their private account, subject to the condition; that those privileged articles should be lodged in the warehouses of the Company, that they should be exposed by them at their sales, and that they should pay from 7 to 5 per cent. to cover the charge of commission and merchandise.

The Act of 1793, relieved the trade carried on under this indulgence, by reducing the rates of charge to 3 per cent.; which was established as the rate, at which the more enlarged trade, for the first time allowed by that Act to private merchants unconnected with the Company, should pay to the Company; which trade was then limited to 3000 tons, the shipping for which was to be provided by the Company, who were to be paid freight for such tonnage, and were to have the same control over the goods which might be imported, as they already exercised over the trade of their Captains and Officers.

It was soon found, that the conditions, under which this trade was opened, changed its operations, so as to render the privilege of little value. The residents in India, for whose benefit it was professed to have been principally intended, presented memorials upon the subject to the Governments abroad; and the merchants of London represented to the authorities in England, the necessity of an enlargement of the principle, as well as a correction of the regulations. It is not necessary, to go into any detail of the reasons upon which those applications were supported; because Mr. Dundas, who then presided over the affairs of India, and who had introduced and carried through Parliament the Bill of 1793, did in the most explicit terms inform the Court of Directors, in his letter of the 2d April, 1800, that "he should be uncandid, if he did not fairly acknowledge, that experience had proved it to be inadequate to the purposes for which it was intended—and that therefore he was clear, that the clause in the Act ought to be repealed, and in place thereof *a power be given to the Governments abroad, to allow the British subjects, resident in India, to bring home their funds to Britain on the shipping of the country;*" that is to say, on ships built in India. This letter, of the President of the Board of Control, was referred by the Court of Directors to a special Committee of their body; who, in a very elaborate Report, dated 27th Jan. 1801, that is to say, after the deliberation of eight months, declared that it was impossible for them to acquiesce in the proposition then made by Mr. Dundas. They supported their opposition by a variety of arguments, from which the following short passage need alone be selected:—"The proposals which have been brought forward by certain descriptions of men, both in India and in England, for the admission of their ships into the trade and navigation between India and Europe, *proposals which extend to the establishment of a regular and systematic privilege* in favour of such ships, appear, when maturely weighed, and followed into all their operations, *to involve principles and effects dangerous to the interests both of the Company and of the nation;* that *the adoption of those principles would, immediately and essentially, affect both the system of policy which the Legislature has established for maintaining the connexion and communication between this country and British India, and the chartered privileges of the East India Company*. And the introduction of any practice of this nature, would tend to widen gradually, and indefinitely, the channel of intercourse between India and Britain; to multiply the relations between the two countries; and to pour Europeans of the lower sort into India, and Indian sailors into this country; to lessen, by both these means, the respect for the European character; *to disturb and shake our government there*; and, in a word, to lead progressively but surely to colonization."

The language employed by the Court of Directors at the present day, in opposition to the proposition for allowing private ships returning from India to import to the places from whence they had sailed upon their outward voyage, is feeble and languid; in comparison with the passage which has been just now recited, from the Report of their Special Committee, made upwards of twelve years ago, upon the proposition then submitted by Mr. DUNDAS. That Minister, in his reply of the 21st March, 1801, to the Court of Directors, observed, "*I have reviewed my own opinions with the most jealous attention, and I have weighed, with the most anxious care, the arguments of those who suppose that the system which I have recommended, is likely to produce any inconvenience or danger to the rights, privileges, and exclusive interests of the East India Company: but it is my misfortune to view the subject in an opposite light. If any thing can endanger that Monopoly, it is* AN UNNECESSARY ADHERENCE TO POINTS NOT ESSENTIAL TO ITS EXISTENCE." Mr. Dundas then adverted to a letter of the 30th September, recently received from the Governor-General, Marquis Wellesley, which, he said, "had with clearness and precision ably detailed and demonstrated the grounds of those opinions."

But, the judgment and reasoning of Mr. Dundas, elucidated by the arguments of Marquis Wellesley, (which were founded on the knowledge of what, at the time, was passing under the eye of the Governor-General,) had not influence upon the Court of Directors, sufficient to make them adopt the proposition of the President of the Board of Control; and still less, the enlargement of that proposition, as suggested by Lord Wellesley; who represented, "the great advantages that would result to the Sovereign State, by encouraging the shipping and exportation of India; and, that if the capital of the Merchants in India, should not supply funds sufficient for the conduct of the whole private Export Trade from India to Europe, no dangerous consequences could result from applying, to this branch of commerce, capital drawn directly from the British Empire in Europe:" thereby taking that trade from foreign nations, whose participation in it was become *"alarmingly increasing."*

These distinct and concurring opinions, of the President of the Board of Control and the Governor-General, could not prevail upon the Court of Directors to "alter the opinion they had delivered." They accordingly drew up paragraphs, to be sent to the Governments in India, conveying their *final resolutions and instructions.*—"The British residents in India," they said, "aided by those who take up their cause here (*viz.* the King's Ministers and the Merchants of London), desire to send their own ships to Britain, with private merchandise; and the principle of employing British capital in this trade, is also contended for. This trade, although it might for a time be carried on through the existing forms of the Company, would at length supersede them; the British commerce with India, instead of being, as it is now, *a regulated monopoly,* would deserve, more properly, the character of a regulated free trade; a title, which it is to be feared would not suit it long."

Such is the substance of the paragraphs which the Directors had prepared, upon the propositions we have been considering; although both the one and the other of those propositions explicitly provided, *that all the private trade with India, export as well as import, should be confined to the Port of London.* The Board of Control, though no longer presided at by Mr. Dundas, interposed its authority; and, on the 2d June, 1801, the Directors were enjoined not to send those paragraphs to India.

The language of the Court of Directors in 1813, upon the question of the Import Trade, is, as has been already affirmed, feeble and languid in comparison with that which the same body employed in 1800 and 1801, with regard to the admission of India-built ships in the carrying trade between Britain and India; but Indian-built ships have, from that time to the present, been employed in that trade, and none of the alarming consequences, which the Directors had predicted, have resulted from that practice.

May it not therefore be reasonably assumed, that the alarm under which they now profess themselves to be, would prove to be equally unfounded; that the direful influence upon the Constitution and Empire, which the Directors tell us is to be apprehended, from any change in the existing system that shall admit private ships returning from India to import at the places whence they had cleared out, would be found to be as little entitled to serious consideration; and that neither the public revenue, nor the immediate interests of the Company, would be endangered by an experiment, which the Government and the Company would be equally bound to watch; and which Parliament could at all times control, and if necessary, absolutely bring to a termination?

GRACCHUS.

LETTER IV.

Saturday, Jan. 16, 1813.

Having hitherto taken a view of those parts of the India Question, which more immediately relate, to the commercial interests of this country, and to the Proprietors of East India Stock; let us now advert to the deportment of the Directors towards the Ministers of the Crown, in their last communication made to the Court of Proprietors.

It appears, from the printed papers, that as long back as the month of April, the President of the Board of Control put the Court of Directors in full possession of the *final opinion* of His Majesty's Ministers; concerning the privileges of trade which, they conceived, it would be their duty to submit to Parliament, as the basis of a Charter. Early in the month of December, a deputation from the Court of Directors appears to have been admitted, by special appointment, to a conference; in which it is known to every clerk and messenger about the offices, as well as to every member of that deputation, that the three Secretaries of State, the First Lord of the Treasury, and the Chancellor of the Exchequer attended. And it is equally notorious, that two subsequent meetings were held, between the same parties. We are warranted to infer, from the letter of Lord Buckinghamshire, that the discussions which took place at those several conferences, were declared to be open and unreserved; with a view that the Members of Government, and the Members of the Deputation, might freely, and without restraint of form, deliver their reasons for the opinions which they respectively held.

The impression which the Court of Directors received, from the conduct of the Ministers of the Crown, in those conferences, is manifested in the Letter from the Chairman and Deputy Chairman to the President of the Board of Control, of the 30th December, in which "they return sincere acknowledgments for the attention with which their representations had been listened to, in the various interviews with which they had been honoured by his Lordship, and His Majesty's Ministers, who attended."

In conferences of this nature, and between parties thus relatively circumstanced, all that was to be expected from the Ministers of the Crown was, that they should listen with attention to the representations made to them, and should reply to those representations, so as to command the acknowledgment of the inferior party. If, in the issue, (to use the words of Mr. Dundas to the same authorities in 1801,) "after having reviewed their opinions with the most jealous attention, and after having weighed, with the most anxious care, the arguments brought forward, it was still their misfortune to view the subject in an opposite light" to that which presented itself to the judgment of the Directors; it was not to be expected, that they should surrender their own judgment to that of the Directors, who stood in the anomalous character of defendants and judges in their own cause.

At the time that these conferences were terminated, the Ministers appear to have entertained an expectation, that the subject would not be further agitated, until an official communication should be made upon it from Government. The Court of Directors, however, met on the 18th December, and entered something very like a protest, by anticipation, against the measure, which they knew, (from what appears to have passed at the conferences,) would be the subject of that official communication; and they transmitted it to the India Board. By the irregularity of this proceeding; which bore upon the face of it the appearance of a design, either of intimidating Government from coming to the final decision which they had signified, or of creating a bar against future discussion; they precluded Government from going into any detail of argument, and consequently, the reply of the President of the Board of Control appears to have been principally intended, to convey officially to the Court of Directors that result, which the Members of the Deputation were already in possession of; namely, "those conditions, upon which alone, consistently with their public duty, the King's Servants could submit a proposition to Parliament for the renewal of the Charter."

To this official communication, the Chairman and Deputy Chairman of the East India Company sent a reply, wherein they offer some explanation of the irregularity; but, in their opposition to the ultimate determination of Government, they call upon the King's confidential servants, to impart to them all the reasons which had determined them to think, that "the privilege of Eastern commerce should be extended to British merchants;" and also, the specific regulations which they may propose to adopt, for giving additional security to the revenue against smuggling.

The President of the Board of Control, thus called upon to step out of his sphere, or to admit the Court of Directors to *Cabinet discussions*, was constrained to acquaint them, that "the duty of Ministers had been performed, by communicating to the Company the conditions on which they were disposed to submit the business to Parliament;" at the same time informing them, that they would find most of the reasons, which had determined the judgment of Ministers to yield to the representations of the out-port merchants, stated "in the petitions presented by those merchants to the Houses of Parliament." And he finally referred them, with confidence, to the "justice and wisdom of Parliament, for obtaining a due regard to their interests."

If the Court of Directors did not entertain feelings and views very different from those of the community at large, in consequence of that peculiar position which renders them *defendants, and judges, in their own cause*, they could not fail to contemplate with applause, the temper, patience, and regard to public engagements, which mark the whole proceedings of Government on this arduous occasion. But, being at one and the same moment, petitioners and arbitrators, and having their judgments biassed under those clashing characters, they have not always kept themselves within the capacity, in which alone they can consistently treat with the Government of the country. In their communications with the Servants of the Crown, respecting the renewal of their Charter, all that they are authorized to pretend to, is to have a distinct knowledge of the conditions, on which the Government think they shall be justified in the sight of the country, in proposing to Parliament the renewal of their Charter; and, in the course of obtaining this information, they have experienced the utmost consideration, and have received the most ample and unreserved communications from His Majesty's confidential servants; who have given their attention to every argument urged by those who appeared as representatives of the Court of Directors, and have put them in possession of all the grounds upon which they differ from them in opinion. After having done this, they have discharged their highly responsible duty to the Public; and if *"they have the misfortune to view the subject in an opposite light,"* the Company's records will show them, that this is not the first time a radical difference of opinion had subsisted, concerning their pretensions, between the King's Ministers and the Court of Directors.

Such being the true state of the case, it becomes a subject of grave inquiry, why the Directors, in the Court of Proprietors held at the India House on the 5th instant, took no step whatever for moderating the spirit which was then shown; or for rectifying the false impressions which were there testified, respecting the deportment of His Majesty's Ministers. It does not appear, that any one of the Directors who were parties in those various conferences, in which they acknowledge to the President of the Board of Control that they experienced so much attention, took any forward step to set right the misrepresentations which were delivered; or to repel the charges, implied or declared, of contempt, neglect, encroachment, &c. which were so freely imputed to the Servants of the Crown. But they left the spirit which had improperly been excited, to act by the impulse of an erroneous impression; omitting to render to the Government that justice, which the frankness of their proceedings strongly called for.

A review of the debate at the India House,—with the Directors, either silently withholding what they were enabled to impart in justification of the Government, or by the rhetoric of some of them tending to blow wider the flames of discord,—would almost authorize a suspicion, that the Directors were not displeased at the fever which their silence nourished. It is therefore earnestly to be hoped, for the honour of the East India Company, and more especially for the interest of the Proprietors, that some Director, or other individual, may, at the next General Court, strive to efface the memory of the last; who may call upon the Deputation, to render to the Ministers of the Crown whatever justice is due to them, for their conduct in the late discussions; and who may recommend a revision of the statement, in which they represent to those Ministers, that the terms on which Government have offered to the Company a Charter, are such as may *"leave their dividend unprovided for,"* and *"create a necessity for their going to Parliament!"* For, unless they have brought themselves to a state to suppose, that Ministers and the Public have lost all intelligence, they must know, that both Ministers and the Public are well aware, that they are actually under *a necessity of going to Parliament* for aid, as soon as Parliament shall be assembled; and that, at the present moment, *their dividend* may, in strictness, be considered as *unprovided for*.

GRACCHUS.

LETTER V.

Tuesday, January 19, 1813.

The writers, who have recently undertaken to defend and justify the opposition of the Court of Directors to any extension of the Import Trade from India to the out-ports of the kingdom, have laid a peculiar stress upon an opinion conveyed in that part of Mr. Dundas's Letter of the 2d of April 1800, in which that Minister was considering "the *agents* to be employed at home; to manage the private trade of individuals from India, and to take care of their interests in the cargoes of the returning ships." He states his opinion, that "there is no use of any interference by the Company; that the great interest to be attended to on *the part of the Company*, is, that no goods come from India that are not deposited in the Company's warehouses; and that the goods, so imported, be exposed at the Company's sales, agreeably to the rules prescribed for that purpose."

In taking ground upon any principle, it is necessary to ascertain whether it applies to the case in point. That it was a great interest to the East India Company to watch and control the trade carrying on under their own licenses, is obvious; and this the Company could not effectually do, unless that Trade, on its return from India, was brought under their own eye, and collected within the sphere of their own control; which is confined to the Port of London. But the case, to which this argument is now applied by the advocates for the Company, is so essentially deficient, that the principles appear to be wholly inapplicable. In this *new case*, the extended trade would be carried on, not under *the Company's licenses*, but under *the provision of Parliament*; and the protection and control of that trade would become the care, not of the Company, but of the executive Government. Here then the determination of that trade would be governed, not by the separate interest of the Company (which alone came within the scope of Mr. Dundas's argument), but by the combined interests of the Company and the Public at large. To this *combined interest*, Mr. Dundas's argument was *not* directed; and it is a fallacy in reasoning, to apply a partial argument to a general case.

But, let us grant what these advocates assume; that the opinion here delivered by Mr. Dundas, does really apply to the case in question. May not that have happened at the present day, which actually did happen with regard to the regulations of the Charter of 1793? Might not new light be thrown upon a subject in 1813, which was supposed to have been thoroughly investigated in 1800? And, as the candour and openness of Mr. Dundas caused him, in 1800, to avow, that the provisions of 1793 were *inadequate*, and prompted him strenuously to recommend the adoption of a *new principle*; is it not possible that, taking into his view all the circumstances which bear upon the question at the present day, he might, had his life been spared, have been convinced, that the extraordinary and unforeseen changes which have taken place in the political and commercial world, might have now rendered it, not only expedient but, necessary to relax, in some degree, upon the point of the import trade from India?

At an early period of the present discussion, Ministers appear to have entertained the same maxim, of confining the import trade from India to the Port of London. They were afterwards led, by a full exposition of all the various interests which remonstrated against that close restriction, to deem it just and expedient to propose (and wise and politic for the East India Company to consent), that *such of the principal out-ports as possessed the means whereby smuggling could best be guarded against*, should participate with London in the import trade from India; reserving exclusively to London, the whole of the trade from China. This alteration of their original plan was suggested by them to the Court of Directors, not as a relaxation of the *existing privileges* of the Company (which was the nature of Mr. Dundas's proposition in 1800), but as a qualification to take place under *a new Charter*.

When Mr. Dundas suggested to the Directors the new principle, of admitting Indian-built ships as the vehicle for carrying on the private trade, he was not treating with them concerning *the renewal* of their Charter; for they had then an *unexpired term of fourteen years*, in the privileges conferred upon them by the Act of 1793. His proposition, as has been just observed, went to *a relaxation* of an important part of those *subsisting privileges*; for which he sought to gain their acquiescence; and as his opinion was decided and avowed, "that the ostensible form of Government for India, with all its consequent detail of patronage, must remain as it now is, and that the monopoly of that trade ought properly to continue in the hands of the East India Company;" it was prudent and seasonable in him to dwell upon that point.

Have not the Ministers of the present day evinced the same opinion? Have they not proposed, to leave the patronage of India, and the exclusive profits of the China Trade, with the Company? Does not the China Trade ensure the employment of all the large ships in the service of the Company; together with the continued engagement, in that line of service, of the Commanders and Officers of those ships; and also, of every other description of person now connected with that (*the largest*) branch of the Company's concerns? Have not Ministers proposed to confine the private trade with India to ships of four hundred tons and upwards; thereby leaving to the owners of such of the smaller ships now in the service of the Company, as by possibility may not be required for their commerce, the advantage (which establishment in any line of business must always give) of finding employment from those who, under the proposed extension, may engage in that trade? Have not Ministers, in proposing that the *Government* of India should continue to be administered through the organ of the Company, proposed to them the continuance of the peculiar and great benefit, of carrying on their *commerce* by means of *the revenue* of that Government? Whereas, the private adventurers must trade upon their own capitals, or at an heavy charge of interest.

How is it, then, that we hear so much of the loss which our Navy must sustain, from the large ships of the Company being withdrawn from the Eastern Trade; of the distress to which the Commanders and Officers, and the numerous classes of artificers and others connected with those ships, are to be exposed? Why are we told, that the East India Docks will be left empty, and the Proprietors be reduced to apply to Parliament for an indemnification? Can it possibly happen, that all these calamities, so heavily denounced, should arise out of a permission to be granted to private ships, returning from India, to proceed to *certain ports to be designated;* more advantageously situated for their trade than the Port of London? A permission, which the Directors themselves are of opinion will not long be made use of to any great extent; for they have told us, that the adventurers in those private ships will be disappointed in their speculations; and they have adverted to the mass of individual loss, which must ensue from the delusion, as furnishing a strong argument, why Government ought not to yield to the importunity of the Merchants of the out-ports.

From all that has been stated, it would appear, that instead of the exaggerated picture of distress, which the advocates for a close monopoly to the Port of London have represented as the necessary consequence of relieving commerce from its present restrictions, we ought to entertain a well-founded expectation; that *every class and description of persons,* who now find employment in the Indian Trade, will continue to have their industry called into action in the same line of employment, and even to a greater extent, in some instances, than is now experienced. For, unless the *union of interests,* which has so recently taken place between the City of London and the East India Company, should have the effect of preventing all competition between the Merchants of London (formerly so eager to participate in the trade with India), and the Merchants of the out-ports; it cannot fail to happen, from the spirit of enterprise which has uniformly distinguished the Metropolis, that the Port of London, *to which the whole India Trade would be generally open,* will furnish its full proportion of the new adventurers; and thus amply fill up that void, which the East India Company affirm would be created in the Port of London, by diverting so much of the Indian Trade to the out-ports: more especially, as all the houses of Indian agency, which have been formed since the Act of 1793, are established within the Metropolis.

Since this is the just prospect, which the adoption of the conditions proposed by Government as the terms for the renewal of the Company's Charter, opens to our view; since the share which the London Merchants may take in the enlargement of the trade, would not fail to supply employment for all that industry, which the Court of Directors assert will be interrupted and suspended; while, at the same time, the extension of that advantage will create new sources of industry in various parts of the kingdom, without impairing or diminishing that of London; whose will be the awful responsibility, if, by an obstinate rejection of terms capable of yielding consequences so extensively beneficial to the community, the Charter of the Company should not be renewed; and if the disastrous effect should in consequence be produced, in London and its vicinity, of "a suspended industry, interrupted employment," and all the train of sufferings and calamities which has been drawn out? Who will be chargeable, before the country, with "the loss and waste of establishments which have cost upwards of a million sterling—of shipping, to the amount of many millions—of a numerous and respectable class of warehouse-keepers, clerks, and superior servants, joined to three thousand labourers, and their families—of tradesmen of various descriptions, who have incurred a very great expense for the conduct of their business?" Who will be chargeable, in fact, with all this destruction? Will it be the Government, who desire the East India Company *to keep their Indian Empire, and their exclusive China trade*? Or will it be the Conductors of the East India Company, who shall suffer this great machine suddenly to stop its action, *because their limited exclusive privileges are not made perpetual*?

GRACCHUS.

LETTER VI.

Friday, January 22, 1813.

Gracchus is charged, by some of the champions of the East India Company, with error and a want of candour, because he has represented the Directors to have maintained, that opening the import trade from India to the out-ports of the kingdom, involves a question of the last importance to the British Empire in India, and to the British Constitution at home; and those writers affirm, that the Directors do not deduce the danger of those great interests from the question of the out-port trade, but from the question of disturbing the present system of administering the Government of India.

Yet he can discover, neither error nor want of candour in his statement. If those advocates will take the pains to follow the whole argument of the Directors, on the present occasion, throughout, they must be sensible, that his statement cannot be controverted. The Directors, indeed, avoid expressing their proposition in the fair and distinct form in which it is here drawn out; yet such is the proposition in effect. For, if the whole of it be reduced into a form of syllogism, it is no other than this:—

> "Whatever shall cause the subversion of the present system of Indian Government, will cause danger to the Empire and Constitution.
>
> "But, pressing the extension of *an import trade from India to the out-ports*, will cause the subversion of the present system of Indian Government.
>
> "Therefore, *pressing the extension of an import trade to the out-ports, will cause danger to the Empire and Constitution.*"

If we question the *minor* proposition, and ask, Why, pressing an import trade for the out-ports, should necessarily cause the subversion of the existing system of Indian Government? the answer of the Directors is already given:—Because they *will not* continue to carry on that Government, if an import trade from India should be granted to the out-ports. Thus, the original statement is demonstrably established; and all the logic of the City cannot overturn it.

The Directors must permit the words *"will not;"* for, with the record of the East India Company's history before us, it is impossible to say they *cannot*. In proof of this assertion, let us take a review of that history, and let us examine, what evil resulted to the Company, *during the period that the import trade from India* WAS ACTUALLY *extended to the out-ports of Great Britain*.

When the first, or London East India Company, had incurred the forfeiture of their Charter in 1693, by the non-payment of a stipulated sum of money, their privileges were immediately restored to them, and confirmed by letters patent, granted by King William III. upon this express ground:—"Considering how highly it imports the honour and welfare of this our kingdom, and our subjects thereof, that a trade and traffic to the East Indies should be continued; and being well satisfied that the same may be of great and public advantage; and being also desirous to render the same, as much as in us lies, *more national, general, and extensive, than hitherto it hath been,"* &c.

This principle, of promoting a more national, general, and extensive trade to India than had subsisted under the then existing Company's exclusive Charter, gave rise to *a new measure* in the year 1698, in an Act passed in the 9th and 10th year of the same king, entitled, *An Act for raising a sum not exceeding two millions, &c. and for settling the trade to the East Indies*. The parties subscribing towards that loan, were formed into a Society, called *The General Society of Merchants, &c.*; and such of them as chose to unite their subscriptions, and to form a joint-stock, were incorporated under the name of *The English East India Company, &c.* The General Society possessed the privilege of an export and import trade with India, with the power of *bringing their import cargoes from India to the* OUT-PORTS *of the kingdom*, in the same manner as is proposed by Government at the present day; with this only difference, that the General Society of Merchants were not restricted as to the ports at which they should enter, whereas Government have *now* proposed, that merchants *should be restricted to such ports as can best afford the means of guarding against the depredations of smuggling*.

The regulations, which were adopted for ships importing from India to the out-ports, are to be found in the Act 9 and 10 William III. c. 44. s. 69. and were as follows:—

> "Provided always, and it is here enacted, that no Company, or *particular person or persons*, who shall have a right, in pursuance of this Act, to trade to the East Indies, or other parts within the limits aforesaid, shall be allowed to trade, until *sufficient security* shall be first given (which the Commissioners of the Customs in England, or any three or more of them for the time being, are hereby authorized and required to take, in the name and to the use of His Majesty, his heirs and successors), that such Company, or *particular persons*, shall cause all the goods, wares, merchandise, and commodities, which shall at any time or times hereafter, during the continuance of this Act, be laden by or for them, or *any of them*, or for their, or any of their accounts, in *any ship* or ships whatsoever, bound from the said East Indies, or parts within the limits aforesaid, to be brought (without breaking bulk), to *some port of England or Wales*, and *there be unladen and put to land*, &c. And that all goods and merchandises belonging to the Company aforesaid, or *any other traders to the East Indies*, and which shall be *imported into England or Wales*, as aforesaid, pursuant to this Act,

> shall by them be sold openly and publicly, by inch of candle, *upon their respective accounts*, and not otherwise."

Upon this Act of the 9th and 10th of William III. was built, in the following year, that famous Charter of the Company, upon which they rest the weight of their pretensions; and that very Charter, as is here rendered incontestable by the Act itself, comprehended the principle, *of an Import Trade from India to the* OUT-PORTS *of the kingdom*.

The form and condition of the security which was to be given by the out-port merchants, will be found in the Act, 6th Anne, c. 3. entitled, *"An Act for better securing the duties on East India goods."* By that Act, the security to be given was fixed "at the rate of 2500*l.* sterling for every hundred ton their ships or vessels shall be respectively let for;" and the *only* restriction imposed upon the import trade from India was, that it should be brought *"to some port in Great Britain."*

Thus, then, any man who looks but a little beyond the objects which lie accidentally before his eyes, may see, that the measure now suggested by Government, instead of being a wild and airy speculation, a theoretical innovation, a *new*, untried, and dangerous experiment, on which we have no ground to reason from experience (as it has been ignorantly and falsely asserted), is nothing more than reverting to an *ancient* principle, involved in the Company's applauded Charter of the 10th of William the Third, and to the practice of our forefathers in the brightest period of our domestic history; a period, in which the British Constitution received its last perfection, and from which the present power and greatness of the British Empire, in the East and in the West, dates its origin.

Having sufficiently proved and established this *great fact*, let us next inquire, what history reveals to us, of *the consequences* of that import trade to the out-ports, that can tend, in any degree, to justify, or give support to, the Company, in determining to resort to an alternative which, they acknowledge, will subvert the system of Indian Government (and thereby shake the Constitution at home), rather than *renew the measure* of a regulated trade to the out-ports.

We have not to deduce these consequences from *abstract hypothesis*, but from *historical testimony*; let us, then, observe what that testimony unfolds. No evil, of any kind whatever, resulted to the incorporated, or Joint Stock Company, from the privilege enjoyed by the out ports. On the contrary, that *Joint Stock Company*, issuing out of the General Society of Merchants (which, as has been above stated, soon became the English East India Company), rose above all their competitors, notwithstanding the power of importing, without limitation, to *any of the ports of the kingdom*; and such was the rapidity of their progress, that they overcame the former, or London Company; they obtained a surrender of all their rights to St. Helena, Bombay, and all their other islands and settlements in India; they at length received that ancient Company into their own body; and finally became the United East India Company of the present day. And so little did the competition and free import of the general merchants tend to obstruct the growth of the United Company, even in the age of its *infancy*; and so "superior were the advantages they derived from trading with a joint-stock (to use the words of one of the Company's most strenuous champions), that at the time of the union of the two Companies, out of the whole loan of two millions, only 7000*l.* then remained the property of the *separate traders of the General Society*; and this sum also was soon absorbed in the United Company[4]." If then the Company, starting originally with only a joint stock, against a competition in the out-ports of the kingdom, with a power to import to those out-ports, outstripped and overcame all their competitors; what can they seriously apprehend from a renewal of the same experiment, in the present momentum of their power, and when they are able to unite with their joint-stock, the whole of the revenues of their present empire in the East?

But it may be asked, if no better success is likely to attend the commercial speculations of the out-ports, why is so strong an effort made, to admit them to a share in the India trade? The answer is obvious. When Mr. Dundas, in the year 1800, so forcibly expressed his opinion against any such admission, he did not ground that opinion upon a question of *ports*, but of *commercial capital*. He considered the capital of the Company as sufficient for all the advantage which the Public, in the aggregate, could derive from the India Trade; and he maintained, that the aggregate interest of the Public would suffer from any measure, tending "to divert any larger proportion of the commercial capital of the country from a more advantageous and more profitable use." But the circumstances of the world are become materially altered, since the period of 1800. The commercial capital, of which Mr. Dundas then reasoned, is deprived of that advantageous and profitable employment which his argument supposed, and is therefore without application or direction; from whence it has resulted, that the operation of commerce is interrupted, and its activity suspended. The allowing that capital to be partially directed to the markets of India, would therefore, under present circumstances, have the great national advantage, of recovering the activity and spirit of commerce, and of encouraging an extensive public interest which is at present disappointed, if not dormant; and, whenever a more prosperous state of things should return, the capital so engaged for a time, would, from the nature of commerce, unquestionably recall itself, and seek again a more profitable market, if any such should open. In the mean time, the East India Company, adding to their joint-stock all the revenues of India, need hardly know, because they could not *feel*, that they had any competitors in the markets of India. And, as the Executive Government was able to guard the out-ports against smuggling in the period of *the infancy* of the Company, they might and ought to feel a perfect confidence, that the same authority can guard them equally now, in the present period of *their maturity*.

Thus, since history renders it indisputable, that an import trade from India to the out-ports of the kingdom has been heretofore exercised under Acts of Parliament, and that it may be perfectly compatible with the highest prosperity of the East India Company; since the Executive Government can guard it against smuggling at the present day, as well as in the reigns of King William and Queen Anne; and since a great and urgent national interest reasonably demands it, both from Parliament and the Company; the present moment furnishes a most fit occasion for the Company to consider, Mr. Dundas's solemn call upon "their wisdom, pol-

[4] A Short History of the East India Company.

icy, and liberality," made by him to them in the year 1800; and also, his weighty admonition, that *"if any thing can endanger their monopoly, it is* AN UNNECESSARY ADHERENCE TO POINTS NOT ESSENTIAL TO THEIR EXISTENCE."

It has been called *illiberal,* to question the motives of the Directors, in refusing their consent to an import trade to the out-ports. But, with the facts of history, which have been here produced, staring us and them in the face, it would be impossible not to question those motives. No man can entertain a higher respect for the East India Company, as a body politic and corporate, or contemplate with higher admiration the distinguished career which it has run, than Gracchus; but, at the same time, no one is better persuaded of the operation of *policy,* in a body circumstanced as they are. And it is more especially necessary to watch that policy, and to be free to interpret *political motives,* at the present crisis, because, at the eve of the expiration of the Company's *last* Charter, in 1793, certain rights were anxiously alleged on their behalf, in a work entitled, *"A Short History of the East India Company,* &c." rights absolutely unmaintainable, and utterly incompatible with the sovereignty of the Empire, and the freedom of the Constitution; and the allegations then made, appear now to assume the form of *a practical assertion*. To those alleged rights, therefore, it will be advisable early to call the attention of Parliament and of the nation.

GRACCHUS.

LETTER VII.

Wednesday, Jan. 27, 1813.

There is an irritability manifested at the present moment, by those who are intimately united in interest with the East India Company, which appears strongly indicative of an unhealthy case. It is well known, that the revenues of the Company, far from being able to contribute to the revenues of the State that augmentation which was made the condition of the Company's present Charter, have, from causes which the Directors could not control, been so deficient, that they have been obliged, at different times, to apply to Parliament for pecuniary aid; that they are burdened with a debt of not less than forty-two millions; and that they are *now* unable to discharge their engagements, without again coming to Parliament to obtain the means. Yet, "AN OLD PROPRIETOR" feels no uneasiness from this state of the Company's affairs; and this, we must suppose, proceeds from an opinion, that the dividend he now receives is *secured to him for the time to come*.

But Parliament has never, directly nor indirectly, made itself a *collateral security* to the Proprietors, for the payment of a dividend of 10½ percent. The aids, at different times granted by Parliament, have proceeded from a mixed principle, of *equity* and of *liberal support*. Of *equity*, in so far as the embarrassments of the Company have been occasioned by political events; of *liberal support*, in so far as those embarrassments may have been caused by disappointment in trade. If the Proprietors should not discriminate between these two principles which have actuated Parliament, but claim the whole of the succours afforded, upon a ground of *positive right*, they might impose upon Parliament the necessity of requiring the East India Company to bring their affairs to a final settlement; in order that it may be accurately determined, how far the Public are equitably pledged to the Proprietors, and how far the Proprietors must be left to settle their own accounts with the Company alone. And it is possible, that the result might not afford that confidence of a well-secured dividend of ten and a half per cent., which an OLD PROPRIETOR considers it an attack upon private property even to question.

Such an issue, however, does not appear to be very likely to occur, unless the Managers of the East India Company's concerns, from any ill-advised determination in their counsels, should take some steps, by which their affairs should be abruptly brought to a settlement: in which event, any disappointment or loss sustained by the Proprietors will be chargeable upon those Managers, who thus desert their duty to their Constituents; and not on the Public, or the Government. The Managers of the East India Company, having so clear and responsible a duty binding upon them, ought to be most scrupulous of failing in that duty, through any capricious or speculative *"adherence to points not essential to their existence;"* for, if they should sacrifice the interest of the Proprietors by now attempting to convert their *temporary grants* into a *perpetual right;* although the disappointed Proprietors may arraign the Public, yet the Public at large will, with justice, impeach the Managers of the East India Company.

In order to open the eyes of the Proprietors to the simple fact of their actual position, their attention was called by Gracchus, on the 13th inst. to the consideration, whether the Company, loaded with a debt of 42,000,000*l.* and being unable to discharge the sum of four millions becoming due, could reasonably expect, that if Parliament should now come to their immediate relief, it would engage itself, *in all future time,* for the payment of a dividend of ten and a half per cent.; especially, if, upon any contingent winding up of the Company's affairs, called for by their own pertinacity, their remaining resources should be found inadequate to secure that dividend to the Proprietors? And the possible case was suggested, of some guardian of the public purse deeming it equitable, that in the event of Parliament being disposed to come to the relief of the Proprietors, under such circumstances, the latter should be called upon, on their part, to submit to some condition of accommodation.

"An Old Proprietor" discovers in this argument of caution, only *a direct menace* from the Executive Government to the purses of the Proprietors;—a plain and intelligible *threat,* that payment of their just claims shall be withheld; and he "thanks God, that he lives in a country, where such language will be treated with merited scorn." This Old Proprietor should have known, that Government has never declined to settle any accounts with the East India Company, which had been properly authenticated: under present circumstances, it is not to be expected, that Government should incur the responsibility of applying the public money to discharge claims which have not been sufficiently investigated. So far, however, is Government from having evinced any disposition to throw unnecessary difficulties in the way of the Company's pecuniary arrangements, that, in the midst of the present contest with the Directors, it has granted to the Company a suspension of the payment of between 8 and 900,000*l.* of tea duties, which the Company had actually received from the buyers of the tea. It is perhaps not generally known, that the Company formerly paid the duties upon tea upon its being imported and landed; by which means the amount of duties was immediately drawn into the Exchequer. To accommodate the Company, a change of practice was allowed by Government, and the Company have been permitted to sell their teas, in the first instance, without the interference of the Officers of the Customs, upon condition of the Company afterwards remitting the gross amount of duties to the Board of Revenue. Thus they actually make their own profits upon the tea, and receive into their own hands the Government duties, before they are called upon to pay them. The duties actually so received by the Company, amount to the sum above stated; and the *Old Proprietor* will probably deem it no slight proof of a wish on the part of Government to render an accommodation to the Company, that, during the pending discussion, it has made arrangements for allowing the Company an extended period, for transferring the very considerable sum of which they have actually received the beneficial use.

It should be always remembered, by the Company, and by the Public, as parties in a great compact, that the privilege of an exclusive trade to India and China has never been granted to the Company without reserve; or, as if their possession of that exclusive benefit was, *in itself*, the most advantageous arrangement for the public interest. The grant has always proceeded upon a principle, of bargain and covenant; and on the consideration of a pecuniary, advance, to be made by the Company to the Public, as the condition for the renewal of *the lease of the public rights in the India trade*. Upon this principle alone, has the exclusive trade ever been conceded to the East India Company; either under its present form, or under any of its former denominations.

To shorten the discussion, however, let the Proprietors and the Company take the following compressed view, of the probable consequences which would severally result, from a *compliance with*, or *rejection of*, the proposition made by Government, as the basis of a new Charter; and let them consider, in *which of the two* they foresee the greatest security for their own future interests.

If, upon maturely weighing the case before them, the Company should accede to the proposition of Government; and if an arrangement, founded upon that proposition, should receive the sanction of Parliament;

1. The Company will preserve *the entire China trade*; and this principal sphere of their commercial profit, will remain undisturbed.

2. They will possess advantages for continuing to carry on the India trade, so far superior to those of all private competitors, from *their territorial and commercial revenues*, that, with a moderate exertion of their activity, they may preserve almost the whole of that trade.

3. They will possess *the regulation and control of the India trade*, so far as depends upon the Indian Governments; and as those Governments will continue in the exercise of the executive power, all the private Merchants, who may repair to the ports and harbours within the extensive limits of their jurisdiction, will of course *be subject to the authority of their Government*.

4. They will retain the whole patronage and expenditure of a revenue of upwards of *Fifteen Millions* sterling per annum in India, together with very extensive establishments at home, depending upon that revenue.

5. The accounts between the Public and the Company, being brought to no sudden and violent crisis of settlement, may be amicably and leisurely adjusted, with a view to mutual convenience.

On the other hand, should the Company incautiously drop the *substance* to pursue the *shadow*, and refuse the proposition of Government; and should Parliament, upon a full and deliberate consideration of the actual circumstances of the Company, deem it more advisable to bring their accounts with the Public to a thorough investigation and final settlement, than to admit the Company's new pretensions to *a perpetual monopoly*;

1. The Company will lose as much of the China trade as may fall into the

hands of the private merchants, who *think* they shall be able to sell tea 85 per cent. cheaper than the Company.

2. They will lose the control of the India commerce, *and will carry on their traffic in India as subjects,* in common with the private British merchants.

3. By that loss, voluntarily incurred, they may throw the greatest part of the trade into the hands of the private traders.

4. They will *lose the patronage of India, and the establishments depending upon it;* which they will thus compel Parliament, contrary to the disposition of Government, to place under different arrangements.

5. The accounts between the Public and the Company must be referred for investigation to Commissioners of Inquiry, to be finally settled and adjusted.

It is now for the Proprietors, after well considering these two alternatives, to determine, under *which of the two* their dividend will be *most secure.*

With regard to Constitutional objections against taking the Government of India out of the hands of the Company (upon which objection their confidence in their present pretensions chiefly reposes), it is difficult to conceive that the wisdom of Parliament, after the experience of so many years, is unequal to the task of devising a system as good as that of the Company, without incurring the evil which those Constitutional objections suppose. The Company's Government, it must be recollected, has been a production of chance, and has grown by the progress of accidental events. It has, indeed, answered far better in practice than could have been expected, if we consider its origin; and therefore, it is not desirable that it should be materially altered; neither is it likely that any such alteration of the system should be contemplated, unless the indiscretion of the Company should impose upon Parliament the necessity of resorting to that measure. But it certainly does not seem to be a measure insuperably difficult, to preserve whatever is really good in the present system, and even to remedy some of its defects, without departing from the path of experience, and resorting to improvements of theory and experiment.

There is one point of view, however, in which such a system would acquire an evident advantage over that which has hitherto obtained: viz. that it would, in every Session, be liable to the revision of Parliament, and to the immediate correction of every error which might be observed, and to such further continual improvements as experience might direct; *not being embarrassed by the compact of a Charter.*

GRACCHUS.

LETTER VIII.

Wednesday, February 17, 1813.

It is very observable, that the objections which have been made by the East India Company to the admission of ships, returning from India, to import and dispose of their cargoes at any other place than the Port of London, are not founded so much upon any statement of the injury which the trade of the Company would sustain by admitting them, as upon a provident regard for the adventurers themselves, and a caution held out to them not to entertain an expectation of benefiting by any commercial speculation in India; since the long experience of the Company has enabled them to show, that it must be ultimately ruinous to the speculator. The sum of the experience, alleged by those who have come forward to defend this point, is, "*That it is not practicable to extend the consumption of European manufactures generally in India;*" and the facts which they have asserted in support of this experimental argument, and upon which they rest its strength, are these four following:

> 1. That the natives of India entertain a strong characteristic aversion, to engage in commercial transactions with foreigners.
>
> 2. That their religious prejudices, customs, habits, and tastes, render it impossible that they should ever become consumers of our manufactures, to any extent.
>
> 3. That their poverty opposes an insuperable bar to such consumption.
>
> 4. That these facts and their consequences are demonstrated in the examples of the Portuguese and the Dutch, who were not able to carry their export commerce with India to any considerable extent.

Let us take these several propositions in their order; and examine, how far they possess that force of truth, which the Company has supposed to belong to them.

1. In the infancy of the European intercourse with India, the sole object of those who engaged in its commerce was, to procure the produce and commodities of the East. In this pursuit, so far were the natives from opposing any obstacles to their endeavours, that they were found disposed to afford every facility to a traffic, which brought them *specie* in exchange for their manufactures, and for the productions of their soil. This fact, which is established by every writer who treated upon the subject of the India commerce during that period, would of itself constitute a complete answer to those who advance the proposition, that the natives of India

are averse, through an established prejudice, to engage in commercial transactions with foreigners.

When the ingenuity of the French and German artists enabled the speculators in this traffic to introduce *works of fancy*, we learn from Tavernier, who made six several journeys, between the years 1645 and 1670, from France to India, by various routes, that the Rajahs of Hindostan and of the Deccan, as well as the Mahomedan princes of those countries, admitted him into their states; that the articles of manufacture which he introduced were received and purchased with an avidity which encouraged him to continue, for so many years, the pursuit of that commerce; that he found the natives of India, spread over the whole range of country from the Indus to the Caspian Sea, engaged in the active prosecution of foreign traffic; and that the number of *Banyans* (the chief commercial cast of Hindoos) at that time established at Ispahan, were not less than ten thousand. Forster, who, in a more recent period, followed Tavernier in one of the routes which he had traversed, informs us, that, in the year 1783, he found Banyans established at Astrachan, within the Russian empire. And we further learn from Bruce, that the principal agents of commerce at Mocha and Jedda, in the Red Sea, were Banyans; and that they had even extended themselves into Abyssinia. No stronger evidence, therefore, can be required to make it manifest, that foreign as well as internal trade has been in all ages, and still continues to be at the present day, a common practice, and a favourite pursuit of the Hindoos.

2. With regard to the restrictive operation of the religious prejudices and customs of the Hindoos, against the adoption of foreign articles of manufacture; Mr. Colebrooke, lately a Member of the Supreme Council, and an eminent Oriental scholar, has furnished us with information upon this subject, equally important and decisive. In an unpublished work, on the Agriculture and Commerce of Bengal, cited in *The Edinburgh Review*, for November 1812, that gentleman observes, that, according to the sentiments of the Hindoos, "All things come *undefiled* from *the shop*;" or, in the words of Menu, "The hands of an artist employed in his art are always pure; and so is every vendible commodity when exposed to sale: that woollens are purified by a single exposure to air, while water is necessary to purify other clothes." Proceeding with these principles, he further informs us, "That the rainy season and winter of India afford real occasion for the use of woollens; that the fabrics of Europe are always preferred; and, if the articles were adapted in the manufacture to the Indian use, and the price reduced, the consumption would descend from the middle even to the more numerous classes. That the natives of India do not want a taste for porcelaine, and other elegant wares; that they require vast quantities of metallic vessels, and of hardware; that, considering the greatness of the population, and the disposition of the natives to use European manufactures, it cannot be doubted, that a great vend might be found, and that the demand will increase with the restoration of wealth."

The authority of Mr. Colebrooke on this subject would be conclusive, even if it stood alone: but it may be supported by a reference to the opinion of many persons, who have been resident in the great cities of India. Those persons would be found to testify, that at Delhi, at Lucknow, at Hydrabad, Mysore, and Tanjore, in all the capitals, whether Hindoo or Mahomedan, a taste prevails amongst the natives for a variety of articles of European manufacture. The late Nabob of Oude, was known to have affected the European dress; as may be seen by the costume of his picture, in the possession of the Marquis Wellesley.

A large assortment of cut glass lustres has been provided by order, for the Soubahdar of the Deccan; and a person is now proceeding to India, with the license of the Company, for the express purpose of arranging them, when they shall have reached his palace of Hydrabad.

The Rajah of Mysore (and, in the same manner, many of the Serdars of that state), is frequently clothed in scarlet cloth; his servants are generally dressed in woollen of that colour; and he often travels in an English carriage, driven by postillions, who are habited in the English costume. The Rajah of Tanjore exhibits in his palace a colossal marble statue of himself, wrought by the hand of Flaxman; and the monument of his revered Mentor, the late celebrated missionary Swartz, sculptured by the same eminent artist, was executed and sent to Tanjore, at the express and urgent desire of that enlightened Prince.

We must further observe, that so far are the religious and civil habits of the Hindoos from obstructing the intercourse of trade, that their policy has connected trade with religion; and the great festivals of their worship, are at the same time the appointed periods and scenes of their most active commerce. Jaggernaut, Ramisseram, Tripetty, are the most celebrated places of Hindoo devotion within the British dominions; and every one who has resided in India must know, that *fairs* are held at those places at the periods, when the greatest concourse of pilgrims is drawn to them by the celebration of their religious rites and ceremonies. In further illustration of the disposition of the natives to traffic, in every way by which profit can be derived, the following fact may be stated; which can be attested by every officer who served with the army under Sir Arthur Wellesley (now Marquis of Wellington), against the Mahrattas, in 1803. The distant and severe service in which that army had been engaged, had exhausted the store of European necessaries with which it had advanced against the enemy; and the officers arrived at Poonah, almost destitute of those comforts and accommodations. But they found the native merchants of that capital provided with the most essential of those several articles, and they were soon supplied, through the agency of those merchants, with every thing for which they had occasion. Poonah is the capital of a Brahmin government; and, therefore, this single fact would serve to furnish a complete answer to every thing that has been asserted, against the practicability of introducing and extending the manufactures of Europe into every part of Hindostan.

3. That the poverty of a large majority of the native subjects of our Indian Empire is such, as to disable them from acquiring our manufactures, is certainly true; but it is no less true, that a very considerable portion of that population possess the means of indulging in every article of convenience and luxury, both native and European. It has been very generally stated, that there are only *two* classes of people in India, the very rich and the very poor. But a minute investigation into the society of India, would discover the error of this statement, and would show, that there exists a third and *middle* class, far removed from the condition of either

of the others; greatly exceeding in number the former of these, and falling far short of the latter. This class, as they certainly possess the means, would, if proper steps were taken, materially contribute to the demand and consumption of many of our home manufactures.

4. With respect to the evidence, attempted to be drawn from the ill success of the Portuguese and Dutch traders, we are to observe, that the situation of the Portuguese and the Dutch, during the period when they were in possession of the European trade with India, was so exceedingly different from that of the British nation at the present moment, that it is scarcely possible to draw a sound comparison between them. The native Governments were at that time powerful; and the establishments of the Portuguese, and afterwards of the Dutch, extended but a short distance from the sea-coast; the manufactures of Europe were, in a manner, in their infancy; and neither Portugal nor Holland were manufacturing countries. Whereas, the British empire is now established over the richest and most populous regions of India, and its influence is extended even further than its dominion; the manufactures of the United Kingdom have attained a degree of perfection, which never has been equalled; they can be fashioned to the tastes, the wants, and the caprices of every nation and climate; and certainly, the interests of the country call for the cultivation of every channel, which can be opened for the enlargement of our commerce.

We cannot better conclude these observations, than by applying the circumstantial evidence which they afford, to Mr. Dundas's letter of the 2d April 1800; in which that Minister admitted the fact, of a *progressively increasing* consumption; but, at the same time, conceived, that the *customs of the natives* would prescribe *limits* to its extension. "I do not mean to say," says he, "that the exports from this country to India have not been *very considerably increased of late years*; and I make no doubt that, from recent circumstances, *they may be still considerably increased*. But the prospect, *from the causes I have already referred to*, must always be a limited one." What these causes are he thus explains:—"The export trade to India can never be extended to any degree, proportionate to the wealth and population of the Indian Empire; neither can the returns upon it be very profitable to individuals. Those who attend to *the manners, the manufactures, the food, the raiment, the moral and religious prejudices of that country*, can be at no loss to trace *the causes* why this proposition must be *a true one*."

The evidence which has been produced demonstrates, that neither the manners, raiments, nor prejudices of Hindostan, are of a nature to impede the introduction of articles of European manufacture; and it thus proves, that *the causes* assigned for the limitation of our export trade, are not calculated to impose any such limitation. What, then, it may be asked, are the causes, why the consumption of the manufactures of Europe in India has in no degree kept pace with the extension of our territories, and of their population? The examination of this branch of our subject would carry us to too great a length on the present occasion, and will therefore best be reserved for a separate communication.

GRACCHUS.

LETTER IX.

Saturday, March 20, 1813.

In searching for the *causes*, which have prevented an extensive introduction of the British manufactures into the countries subject to the dominion or influence of the British Crown in India, it naturally occurs; that no measure appears ever to have been concerted, for the general purpose of alluring the attention of the natives of India to the articles of European importation. This neglect, has evidently arisen from the opinions which have been so erroneously entertained, concerning the civil and religious prejudices of the Hindoos.

The evidence of Mr. Colebrooke has been adduced, to prove that those opinions are wholly unfounded; the following extracts from the Travels of Forster, in the years 1782-3, will further evince, that the Hindoos, far from entertaining any indisposition to engage in commercial dealings with strangers, have widely extended themselves in different foreign countries for that express purpose.

Herat.—"At Herat, I found in two Karavanseras about one hundred Hindoo merchants, who, by the maintenance of a brisk commerce, and by extending a long chain of credit, have become valuable subjects to the Government. When the Hindoos cross the Attock, they usually put on the dress of a northern Asiatic, being seldom seen without a long cloth coat, and a high cap[5]."

Turshish.:—"About one hundred Hindoo families, from Moultan and Jessilmere, are established in this town, which is the extreme limit of their emigration on this side of Persia. They occupy a quarter in which no Mahomedan is permitted to reside; and I was not a little surprised to see those of the Bramin sect distinguished by the appellation of *Peerzadah*, a title which the Mahomedans usually bestow on the descendants of their Prophet. Small companies of Hindoos are also settled at Meschid, Yezd, Kachin, Casbin, and some parts of the Caspian shore; and more extensive societies are established in the different parts of the Persian Gulf, where they maintain a navigable commerce with the western coast of India[6]."

Baku.—"A society of Moultan Hindoos, which has long been established at Baku, contributes largely to the circulation of its commerce; and, with the Armenians, they may be accounted the principal merchants of Shirwan. The Hindoos of this quarter usually embark at Tatta, a large insular town in the lower tract of the Indus; whence they proceed to Bassorah, and thence accompany the caravans, which are frequently passing into Persia: some also travel inland to the Caspian Sea, by the road of Candahar and Herat. I must here mention, that we brought

[5] Forster's Travels, p. 135-6.

[6] P. 166.

from Baku five Hindoos; two of them were merchants of Moultan, and three were mendicants, a father, his son, and a Sunyassee (the name of a religious sect of Hindoos, chiefly of the Brahmin tribe). The Hindoos had supplied the little wants of the latter, and recommended him *to their agents in Russia*, whence, he said, he should like to proceed with me to England. The Moultanee Hindoos were going to Astrachan, merely on a commercial adventure[7]."

ASTRACHAN.—"The Hindoos also enjoy at Astrachan every fair indulgence. They are not stationary residents, nor do they keep any of their females in this city; but, after accumulating a certain property, they return to India, and are succeeded by other adventurers. Being a mercantile sect of their nation, and occupied in a desultory species of traffic, they have neglected to preserve any record of their first settlement, and subsequent progress, in this quarter of Russia; nor is the fact ascertained, with any accuracy, by the natives of Astrachan[8]."

Having thus seen, that the natives of India are in no respect averse to engage in commercial dealings with strangers, and that no prejudices exist among them of a nature to prevent them from using our manufactures; we cannot but be forcibly struck with the reflection, that no systematic plan has ever been adopted by the East India Company, to attract the attention of the Hindoos to the various articles of our home manufacture, or to stimulate their speculation in the traffic of them. Whereas, in Europe, the Company have always found it necessary, for the disposal of their Indian Imports, to take active measures for drawing the attention of the nations of the European Continent to their sales in London.

The Directors, in their letter to Lord Buckinghamshire, under date of the 15th of April, 1812, (adverting to their sales in Europe,) observe, "That the Foreign Buyers repose confidence in the regularity and publicity with which the Company's sales are conducted; that the particulars of their cargoes are published immediately on the arrival of the ships, and distributed all over the Continent. That notices of the quantities to be sold, and periods of sale, are also published for general distribution; and that the sales of each description of goods are made at stated periods, twice in the year."

No measure of this nature has ever been projected for India; and yet, the predilection of the natives of India, both Hindoo and Mahomedan, for public shows, scenes of general resort, and exhibitions of every kind, is so well known, that we may confidently affirm, that nothing could have a surer tendency to draw them together, than a display, at periodical fairs, of our various manufactures. Fairs of this kind, for the sale of their home manufactures, have been held from time immemorial, in every part of India. The Company, therefore, needed only to engraft, upon an established usage of the Hindoos, a regular plan of periodical fairs; and, by thus adopting in India a course analogous to that which they have found it necessary to employ in Europe, they might generally have arrived at giving to Calcutta, Madras, and Bombay, attractions of curiosity and mercantile interest, which would most probably have drawn to those settlements the wealthy natives from every part of the East; and have rendered the capital cities of British India, what Amster-

[7] Forster's Travels, p. 228.

[8] Forster's Travels, p. 259.

dam, Frankfort, and Leipsic have long been in Europe, the resorts of all descriptions of people, and the repositories of every European article of use and luxury. From these different centres of commerce, the markets of the interior of India, and especially those held at the scenes of religious assembly, might be furnished with supplies; and, under the fostering encouragement of a wise and provident Government, the intelligence and enterprise of the natives of India might be called into action, and be stimulated, by a powerful motive, to exert in their own country those commercial talents that have obtained for them the encouragements, which, upon the unimpeachable testimony of Mr. Forster, they have long received in Persia, and in parts of Russia.

The advantage of collecting together, at stated periods and in established points, the productions of human industry and ingenuity, has been so universally felt by all nations; that there is scarcely a country, advanced to any degree of civilization, in which the practice has not prevailed. To effect this object, with a view to the extension of our export trade in India, *active encouragement* is alone requisite; but, in order to give it stability, *native agency* must be called forth into action. The supplies which (as was mentioned on a former occasion) were found at Poonah, were obtained from that source alone. The Parsee merchants at Bombay, are the principal agents of the Commanders and Officers of the Company's ships; such parts of their investments as are not disposed of among the European population, are purchased, and circulated in the interior, by the Parsees. The small supplies of European manufactures which find their way into the principal cities of the Deccan, proceed from this source: but there is reason to believe, that the articles which arrive at those places are too frequently of an inferior sort, or such as have sustained damage in the transit from Europe.

To give perfection to the great object here sketched out, it will be indispensably necessary that the local authorities in India should direct their most serious attention to this subject. As *our Indian empire is our only security for our Indian trade,* so our Indian trade must be rendered an object of vigilant concern to those who administer the Government of that empire. From the multiplicity and importance of their other avocations, that trade has not hitherto received all the consideration to which its high value is entitled; but, whenever an adequate regard shall be paid to it, it will become a duty of the Governments to take active and effectual steps, for *drawing the attention of the natives to our exported commodities,* and for *promoting the dispersion of those commodities,* within the sphere of their influence or power.

We now discern *one operative cause* of the comparatively small demand for, and consumption of, our European articles, in the Indian empire; a cause, however, which it is within our capacity to control, or to remove. And, after what has been summarily exposed, in this and in the preceding communication, it can be no difficult point to determine, whether *this cause,* or the alleged *prejudices of the Hindoos,* have most contributed to limit the extent of our Export Trade to India.

GRACCHUS.

LETTER X.

THE RIGHTS AND PRETENSIONS OF THE EAST INDIA COMPANY.

Monday, March 8, 1813.

It is now become a matter of the most solemn importance, that the public attention should be called to a clear and deliberate survey of THE RIGHTS and PRETENSIONS of the East India Company; and that the judgment of Parliament should be directed to, and its sense declared upon, the subject of those pretensions, which have generated A NEW CONSTITUTIONAL QUESTION, and are now carried to an height to affect the supreme Sovereignty of the State. To discuss those Rights and Pretensions at large, would demand a far more extended space than the present occasion can supply; but it would be altogether unnecessary to enter into a more enlarged discussion; because, in order to obtain the end here proposed, of drawing and fixing the attention of Parliament and the Public upon the subject, little more is required, than to bring those several Rights and Pretensions into one compressed and distinct point of view; and to leave it to the legislative wisdom to determine finally upon their validity.

The rights of the East India Company, are usually distinguished into their *temporary* rights, and their *perpetual* or *permanent* rights.

I. The temporary rights of the Company are:

1. *A right to the exclusive trade with all the countries lying eastward from the Cape of Good Hope to the Straits of Magellan.* This right is *a lease* of all the *public right* to the trade of those parts of the world; which lease has been renewed to the Company, from time to time, in consideration of a varying premium to be paid by them to the Public.

2. *A right to administer the government and revenue of all the territories in India acquired by them during their term in the exclusive trade.* This is a right delegated from the Crown, with the assent of Parliament; and which can be possessed by the Company no longer, than the authority from which it emanates has, or shall prescribe.

Upon the expiration of these temporary rights, which determine, as the law at present stands, in the ensuing year, 1814, the East India Company will remain in possession of whatever *permanent* rights shall be found to pertain to them.

II. The *perpetual,* or more properly, the *permanent* rights of the Company, must be considered under two distinct heads, viz. *admitted* and *alleged.*

§ 1. The *admitted* permanent rights are,

1. *To be a Body Politic and Corporate, with perpetual succession.*—This right has been confirmed by various succeeding Charters and Statutes. But there are some observations, which it is important to make upon this subject. The first Charter, granted by Queen Elizabeth, in 1601, to the first or London East India Company, created *both its corporate capacity and its exclusive privilege, to continue for a term of fifteen years*; but it provided, that, in case it should not prove beneficial to the Public, the *whole of the grant* might at any time be determined, upon two years notice given to the Company. The succeeding Charters of James I. Charles II. James II. and William and Mary, conferred, in the same manner, both the corporate capacity and the exclusive privilege; and though they did not, like the former, fix a term for their duration, yet they rendered the *whole grant* determinable upon three years notice. No provision is introduced into any of these Charters, to make the corporate capacity outlast the exclusive trade. When the principle of *"a more national, general and extensive trade to India,"* declared in the Charter of the 5th of William and Mary, had been followed by the measure of creating a General Society of Merchants, and of erecting *a New Company*, the advocates for that measure took particular care to show, "That the Old Company, in reciting their Charters, had *forgot* to mention the *provisos* therein, viz. that the respective Kings of England, who granted them, reserved a discretionary power to *make them void* on three years warning[9]." This observation did not apply to their exclusive privilege only, but extended equally to their corporate capacity; both being determinable by the same warning, because both were derived from the same grant, the whole of which grant was made liable to that determination, notwithstanding their corporate capacity was to enjoy *"perpetual succession."* Hence it is manifest, that the perpetuity conferred by the Charter was not perpetuity of exclusive trade, or political power, but of *corporate succession*. But perpetual succession in a body corporate, does not imply perpetuity of duration, but merely *uninterrupted* succession of the individuals who compose it; which every corporate body must possess, whatever may be the term of its duration, in order that it may become, and may be able to perform the acts of, *a legal person*.

The Statute of 9 and 10, and the Charter of 10 William III. which created *both the corporate capacity and the exclusive privilege* of the *New*, or English Company, followed the example of the former Charter, granted to the *Old* Company, and rendered the *whole grant* determinable by the same process. But, in the 10th year of Queen Anne, after the two Companies had become *United*, they represented the great hazard they should encounter, by engaging in any considerable expenses for securing *the Pepper Trade*, under the limitation of that clause; in consequence of which representation the clause was repealed, and the limitation was *left open*. The Company from thence inferred, that they had acquired a perpetuity of duration, both for their corporate capacity and their exclusive privilege; the continuance of *both* of which had ever been subjected to the same rule of determination. They soon, however, became sensible that such could not be the true intention of the Act, and they "submitted themselves to Parliament[10]" on the subject; in consequence of which a limited term of exclusive trade was assigned them, without any

[9] Anderson's Hist. of Commerce (1698), vol. ii. p. 221, fol.

[10] A Short Hist. of the East India Company, p. 6.

limitation being imposed upon the *negative* perpetuity of duration, which they had acquired for their Corporation by the repeal of the determining clause. But it was not till the year 1730, the third year of the late King, that the Company obtained a true and *positive* perpetuity of duration for their Body Corporate; at which time an Act was passed, empowering them to continue to trade to the East Indies, as a Company of Merchants, although their exclusive right to the trade, and their power of administering the government and revenues of India, should be determined by Parliament. From that time only, the Incorporation and the Exclusive Privilege become distinguished. The distinctions here made will be found of material importance, in another part of this statement.

2. *A right to acquire and possess lands, tenements, and property of every kind; and to dispose of the same, under a Common Seal.*—This right was conferred by the Charter of the 10th of King William; but by Stat. 3 G. 2. c. 14. § 14. the Company's estates *in Great Britain* were limited to the value of 10,000*l.* per annum. In virtue of this right, the East India Company were empowered to settle "*factories and plantations,*" within the limits of their exclusive trade. The Charter of William, indeed, adds also "*forts,*" with the power of "*ruling, ordering, and governing them;*" but that this privilege cannot attach upon their corporate and *permanent* capacity, will presently be made to appear. Fortresses and fortifications cannot, from their nature and use, become absolute private property; being part of the public defences of the Empire, they are (to speak with Lord Hale) "*affected with a public interest,* and therefore *cease to be juris privati only*[11]." The building a fort is an act done, in its nature, by virtue of a sovereign authority, and is therefore the dereliction of the private right of property for a public and general purpose. In asserting for the Company a *private* right to forts and fortifications, the Company's advocates have therefore fallen into an extreme error, from not discriminating between the rights which necessarily belong to their *delegated sovereignty*, and those which can alone be annexed to their *commercial corporation*. And this brings us to the consideration of

§ 2. The *alleged* permanent rights of the Company, which require to be considered under *two* descriptions, viz. rights *alleged for them* at the expiration of their last exclusive Charter, and rights *alleged by them* at the present moment, with a view to the renewal of their present Charter. *These* are the rights, or more properly the pretensions, which have been pronounced by Gracchus, "absolutely unmaintainable, and incompatible with the freedom of British subjects;" and not their true legitimate rights, as the writer of a letter under the signature of Probus has chosen to assume.

The rights *alleged for them* were these:—

1. *A right to possess in perpetuity certain extensive territories and seaports in India, after their right to the exclusive trade with those places shall cease.* In consequence of different ancient Charters, granting to the Company an exclusive trade, together with certain powers of Government, they have acquired, and actually possess, various islands, seaports, forts, factories, settlements, districts, and territories in India, together with the island of St. Helena; either by grants from the Crown, by conquest, purchase, or by grants from the native powers in India. The nature and extent of

[11] De Portibus Maris, p. 2. c. 6. p. 77.

their property in these several possessions, is an important public question. By grants from the Crown to the original or London Company, and by conveyance from that Company, they possess St. Helena and Bombay. By purchase, conquest, or by Indian grants, they possess Calcutta and Fort William, Madras, and Fort St. George, and various other important seats of trade; of all of which, for a long course of time; they have enjoyed the exclusive benefit.

With respect to the first of these; it is evident, that the Old Company could only convey the places which they held of the Crown as they themselves held them, and subject to the same principles of policy and state under which they themselves had received them. The Grants of Charles II., which conceded Bombay and St. Helena to the first Company, refer to the Charter of the 13th of the same reign, which Charter refers to, and confirms the preceding Charters of Elizabeth and James I., making them *the ground* of the Grants. The Charter of Elizabeth declares its principle to be, "the tendering the honour of the nation, the wealth of the people, the increase of navigation, the advancement of lawful traffic, and the benefit of the Commonwealth." The principle declared in the Charter of James I. is, "that it will be a very great honour, and in many respects profitable, to THE CROWN and THE COMMONWEALTH." By a reference to, and confirmation of, these several Charters, in the Charter of Charles II., and in the grants of St. Helena and Bombay, these principles are virtually adopted; the *end and purpose of the Grants* is declared; and their ground is proclaimed to be, the honour of the British Crown, and the welfare of the British Nation. It was those great *public interests*, and not the *separate interests* of the Company, that the Crown had in view, in conceding the property of those distant dependencies.

By grants from the native powers, the Company are in actual possession of many extensive and valuable territories. The doctrine of the law of England, in regard to the operation of these Grants, was distinctly and officially declared in the Report of the Attorney-General Mr. Pratt, and Solicitor-General Mr. Charles Yorke, in the year 1757, viz. That the moment the *right of property* vested in the Company by the Indian Grants, the *right of sovereignty* vested necessarily in the Crown of England. "The property of the soil (said those eminent lawyers) vested in the Company by the Indian Grants, *subject only* to Your Majesty's right of sovereignty over the settlements, and over the inhabitants as British subjects; who carry with them Your Majesty's laws, wherever they form colonies, and receive Your Majesty's protection by virtue of your Royal Charters[12]." In considering this head of right, the case of *the five Northern Circars*, to which the Company lay claim in their Petition, demands a particular attention; because, the advocates of the Company's pretensions are under a manifest error, with respect to their tenure of those territories. They maintain, that the Circars are held by the Company in perpetuity, under *a military service*, as tributaries to the Indian Power or Powers by which they were originally ceded; and that the Crown of England has no title to interfere, between them and their supposed Indian Chief. This pretension renders it absolutely necessary, to take a general view of the situation of the Company with respect to the Circars.

[12] Short Hist. of East India Company, p. 11.

In the year 1753, the French were in the confirmed possession of the five Circars, together with the adjoining fort and dependencies of Masulipatam; of all of which they declared themselves to have obtained "*the complete sovereignty for ever,*" by a grant from the Subah of the Deccan, a Prince nominally dependent on the Imperial Crown of the Mogul. "So that these territories (says Mr. Orme), rendered the French masters of the greatest dominion, both in extent and value, that had ever been possessed in Indostan by Europeans, not excepting the Portuguese when at the height of their prosperity[13]." The establishment of the French power in these important provinces, during the war between England and France, excited the most serious alarm in the Company, by threatening their settlements and possessions in Bengal; and called forth the vigorous and splendid exertions of Lord Clive, who, in the year 1759, sent a military force against Conflans, the French Commander, under the command of Colonel Forde. That gallant Officer succeeded in defeating the enemy in a pitched battle at Peddipore; and, pursuing him from one extremity of the Circars to the other, terminated the campaign by the capture of Masulipatam: and thus, by obliging the French to abandon the Circars, the right of conquest was made good against the French. For it is not necessary that every part of a conquered country should be acquired by a separate victory, if the enemy is compelled to evacuate his territory in consequence of any decisive operation; and the retention of Masulipatam, was the evidence of the triumph of the British arms over the French. That this was *the object* of the campaign, is distinctly shown in the declaration made by Lord Clive before the Select Committee of the House of Commons, in the year 1772. Lord Clive stated to the House, "That soon after his appointment of President of the Company's affairs in Bengal, in 1758, he took into his most serious consideration the situation of affairs upon the coast of Coromandel. Monsieur Lally was arrived with such a force, as threatened not only the destruction of all the settlements there, but of all the East India Company's possessions. That he thought it was his duty to contribute his mite towards the destruction of the French, and therefore projected *the scheme of depriving the French of the Northern Circars,* contrary to the inclination of his whole Council. That *this expedition succeeded completely, for the French were totally driven out by* Col. Forde, *with the Company's troops,* whose conduct and gallantry upon that occasion was equal, if not superior, to any thing that had happened during the whole course of the war[14]." This evidence of Lord Clive proves, that the scheme was *entirely military,* and that the success was *the success of arms.* By the Treaty of Peace concluded at Paris in 1763, (Art. 11,) "the Crown of France renounced all pretensions to those territories," which thus devolved, by an indisputable right of conquest, to the Crown of England. The Company, indeed, in the same year obtained a grant of Masulipatam from the Subah of the Deccan, which they now set forth in their Petition to Parliament: but yet, their most strenuous advocates admit, that Masulipatam belongs to the Crown of England, *by right of conquest over the French*[15]. And the same argument, that proves a right of conquest to Masulipatam, proves also a similar right to the Northern Circars.

---

[13] History of Indostan, vol. i. p. 335.

[14] Journals of the House of Commons, vol. xxxiii. p. 811.

[15] Short Hist. of the East India Company.

In 1765, however, the Company being desirous of acquiring *the form of an Indian title* to the Circars, against the Subah, who might reclaim them, negotiated for a grant of those provinces at Delhi, over the head of the Subah; which grant they obtained. But the pretensions of the Subah, who was close at hand, might disturb them in their attempts to occupy the provinces; they therefore thought it *expedient*, to temporize with the Subah, and to enter into a separate negotiation with him, to induce him to surrender them; and they agreed to hold the provinces of him also, under an engagement to supply him with a contingent aid of *military force*, when called upon; and moreover, to pay him annually a tribute in money. By thus confusing their titles (which, instead of confirming, mutually defeated each other), they fully demonstrated the inefficacy and impotency of the Mogul's grant, in the present fallen state of that Empire. But the Company could only engage themselves for *military service*, so far as they possessed the ability; and their ability, is limited by the extent of their *military power*; which, being a part of their *sovereign power*, must necessarily determine with their sovereign capacity: as will be shown in the next article. Whenever that capacity ceases, they will be unable to furnish a single soldier, because they will be unable to raise a single soldier for the defence of the provinces. In that event, the Crown must of necessity interfere, to maintain and defend the territories; and then, *the original cause* which led to the acquirement of the Circars, namely, the expulsion of the French *by force of arms*, and their exclusion by *the influence of the same arms* in the Treaty of 1763, will be the true ground on which to rest *the question of right*: a right in *the Crown of England*, which had existence, prior to *the form* of the Mogul's grant, and prior also to *the expedient* of the grant from the Subah. And here we must keep in mind, that all territories possessed by the Company in India, by whatever means they have been acquired, are necessarily incorporated into the British Empire, and become subject to its Imperial Crown; conformably to the resolution of the House of Commons, in the year 1773: "*That all acquisitions made under the influence of a military force, or by treaty with foreign Princes, do of right belong to the State.*" And as the whole fabric of British India grew out of a principle of advancing *the public welfare*, and was not an edifice raised merely for the separate welfare of *the Company*, every private interest comprehended in that fabric is, by every acknowledged maxim of State, public right, and consistency, subordinate; and must be determined by the security of the public good.

2. *A right to retain in perpetuity certain essential rights of sovereignty, after the present delegated sovereignty of the Company shall have reverted to the Crown.*—Although this pretension is a contradiction in terms, yet the assertors of it entertained no doubts of its reality. They claimed for the Company, in their permanent capacity of a trading body corporate, a right "*to appoint governors, to build and maintain forts, to muster forces by sea and land, to coin money, and to erect Courts of Judicature*[16]," even after they shall have lost their power of administering the Government of India; and this claim is renewed for the Company at the present day[17]. There is in this pretension so radical an ignorance of *the nature of sovereignty*, that it is inconceivable how it could have been entertained by any one, who had ever given

[16] Short Hist. of the East India Company, p. 56.

[17] Morning Post, Jan. 15, 1813, Letter, signed Probus.

a thought to the subject of law or government. The powers here enumerated, are essential prerogatives of sovereignty; which may indeed be delegated for a time by authority of Parliament, but can never be granted in full property by the Crown. In order to appoint governors, it is first necessary to be invested with the power of government. The same power is manifestly necessary, in order to be able *legally to raise or muster any force by sea or land*, either for defence, or for any other military service. And it is acknowledged, that *the power of government* has never been granted to the East India Company, *but with limitation*. In the grants of Bombay and St. Helena, the Company is certainly empowered to erect forts, and to raise and employ forces; but by the same grants they are invested with the powers of Captain General in order to that end; virtually in the first, and *expressly* in the second. Will it be imagined, that they are to retain the authority of *Captain General*, after their powers of *government* shall cease? And if not, it must be evident, that their authority over forts, and all their military power, must determine, whenever their delegated power of Captain General shall determine. It would be an insult to any reader, who has ever cast his eye even on the elementary Commentaries of Sir William Blackstone, to insist upon a truth so obvious and simple. With regard to the *erecting of Courts*, no such power is given in any of the Charters produced in evidence. The Crown erects the Court, and the power granted to the Company is, and necessarily must be, limited and subordinate. The *true cause* of that extraordinary error, is plainly this: the Charters of King William and Queen Anne, upon which they rest these pretensions, conferred at one and the same time (as has been already observed), both their corporate capacity and their exclusive privilege. The assertors of those *permanent sovereign rights*, not discriminating, by the principles of things, between the several powers conferred in those Charters, have confused the provisions; and have construed all the powers above enumerated, which by their nature could only appertain to them as *delegated Sovereigns*, to belong to their capacity of an *incorporated Company*. And, under this illusion, they have imagined, that those powers are annexed to that perpetuity of their corporate body which was first enacted in 1730, and confirmed in the 33d year of the present reign; and that they do not constitute a part of those powers of government, which have been conferred upon them, from time to time, by their exclusive Charters. As this construction is entirely arbitrary on the part of the Company, and as it is unsupported by the principles either of law or sound reason, it will be best refuted by the authority of Parliament.

3. *A right to exclude all British subjects from the Company's Indian ports, after their own exclusive privilege shall be expired.*—This right has been claimed in the following words:—"Although their exclusive right to the trade, and their power of administering the government and revenues of India, were to be determined, they would still remain an incorporated Company *in perpetuity*, with the *exclusive* property and *possession* of Calcutta and Fort William, Madras and Fort St. George, Bombay, Bencoolen, and St. Helena, and various other estates and settlements in India. Whether, in the event of the sole trade being determined, individuals would be able to carry on a successful trade to India, *if the Company were to debar them the use of their ports and factories*, may require a serious consideration[18]."

[18] Short History of the East India Company, p. 38.

This is a claim, not only to a *practical* exclusive trade, after the right to exclusive trade *expressly granted* by Parliament shall cease and determine, but involves also claims of perpetual sovereignty. It is incomprehensible, how it could be alleged by a writer who, in the preceding page, had pointedly excepted from their powers, that of converting the trade into "a *mischievous* monopoly[19];" for, what more *mischievous* form could monopoly, or an hostile sovereignty, assume, than that of excluding all British individuals from the chief ports and seats of trade in India? By this alleged right, the grants of Charters and the provisions of Parliament would be reduced to an absurdity. But as this is a claim of *private right* to cause a *public wrong*, it cannot fail particularly to engage the consideration of Parliament.

The rights *alleged by the Company* at the present day, are these:—

1. *A right to all the ports and territories in India, possessed by the Company, of the same kind and extent as the right by which they hold their freeholds in London.*—This right has been solemnly asserted for the Company, by the Chairman and Deputy Chairman of the Court of Directors, in these words:—"The Company are AS MUCH owners of THE CHIEF SEATS of European trade in the Indian Empire, as they are of THEIR FREEHOLDS IN LONDON[20]." This is an open and unreserved declaration of the East India Company, renewing and asserting the preceding allegations made on their behalf at the expiration of their last exclusive Charter; and the same allegation is now repeated in their Petition to Parliament, though in terms somewhat more qualified than those which they addressed to the Government; viz. "that *no person* can have a right, except with the consent of the proprietors of India stock, *to use the seats of trade* which the stockholders *have acquired*." But they must bring an oblivion over all the reasons of state and policy by which *they exist at all*, before they can carry in the face of the nation the proud assertion, that they stand equally circumstanced, in regard of *private right*, with respect to "*the chief seats of European commerce in the Indian Empire*," and with respect to "*their freeholds in London*." They will assuredly be told by Parliament, that they *may not* exercise the same arbitrary authority over the chief seats of Indian commerce, which they may over their freeholds in London. With regard to their freeholds in London, they may exclude all persons from entering them, they may desert them themselves, or they may let them fall to ruin. But it is NOT SO with regard to the chief seats of Indian commerce; they will find, that they cannot arbitrarily exclude British subjects from those seats, beyond a limited time; that they cannot *debar* the nation the beneficial use of them; and that they will not be suffered to render them unavailable, or unprofitable. As soon as the India Trade shall be thrown open, the ports of India will necessarily become open; and, if the Company should then search for *their private right to close them*, they will find, that it is merged in *the public right to use them*; or, to use the words of Lord Hale, that "their *jus privatum* is clothed and superinduced with a *jus publicum*[21]."

2. The last right *alleged by the Company* at the present crisis, which forms the CLIMAX of their pretensions, and is the *key* to all their late proceedings, is that of

[19] Ibid. p. 37.
[20] Letter to Lord Buckinghamshire, Dec. 30, 1812.
[21] De Portibus Maris, p. 2. c. 7. p. 84.

a *perpetual union and incorporation with the Supreme Government of the Indian Empire;* so that the Indian trade and government must ever continue to be united *in them,* and cannot now be separated, without endangering *"the British Empire in India, and the British Constitution at home."* This pretension renders the question of a *temporary* exclusive trade entirely nugatory, because it is the unqualified assertion of a *perpetual* one; not to be received any more as *a grant* from Parliament, as hitherto it has been, but to be extorted from Parliament through fear of the subversion of Parliament. This pretension is founded upon the Company's interpretation of an observation, made by a late eminent Minister to the Managers of the Company's affairs, in the year 1800; viz. that *"the Government and the trade of India are now so interwoven together,"* as to establish an indissoluble *"connexion of government and trade."* This *dictum,* is assumed by the Company for an incontestable maxim of State, *as applicable to their own Corporation;* and for an eternal principle, connecting that Body Corporate with all future Indian Government. This they denominate, "THE SYSTEM, *by which the relations between Great Britain and the East Indies are now regulated;"* and, in their sanguine hopes of gaining *perpetuity* for their *system,* they already congratulate themselves upon their Incorporation into the Sovereignty, as a NEW, and FOURTH ESTATE of the Empire.

It is that maxim, evidently embraced for this construction at the present crisis, that has emboldened the conductors of the Company's concerns to assume so lofty a demeanour towards the King's servants; and to venture to represent the cautious proceedings of Government in a great political question (in which it appears only as *a moderator* between two conflicting interests), to be an aggression against their indisputable rights. It has been asked in the Court of Proprietors, "whether the Ministers of the present day are become so far exalted above their predecessors, or the Company so newly fallen, that adequate communications should not be made to the latter, of the plans and intentions of the former?" It is neither the one nor the other; but it is, that *the Company* are become so elated and intoxicated by the ambitious expectation of being incorporated as a perpetual Member of the Supreme Government, that they conceive they have no longer any measures to keep with the Ministers of the Crown.

And can the British people *now* fail to open their eyes, and to discern the strait to which the ancient crown and realm of England would be reduced, by submitting to acknowledge this *new estate* in the Empire? Greatly as it would be to be lamented that any thing should disturb the present internal tranquillity of our political system, yet, if such should be the necessary result of a resistance to the ambitious views of the East India Company, it ought to be manfully and cheerfully encountered; rather than admit, by a temporizing concession, a claim which shall bend PARLIAMENT to the will of, and degrade THE CROWN to an alliance with, a Company of its own subjects; which owes its recent existence to the charters of the Crown, and the enactments of Parliament, and yet aspires to seat itself for ever, side by side, by its own supreme Government.

The Company have carried too far their confidence in the *constitutional defence* by which they hoped to ride in triumph over the Executive Government. Their exorbitant pretensions have bred a *new constitutional question,* to which the public mind is now turning. In their solicitude to fortify themselves with *constitutional jealousies*, they have constructed a formidable fortress, which threatens to embarrass the Citadel of the State, and must therefore of necessity awaken its jealousy. A change in the Administration of the Indian Government (should the Company finally provoke such a change), *need not necessarily* throw the patronage of India into the hands of the Crown; means are to be found, by which that political and constitutional evil may be effectually guarded against. But if, through a precipitate assumption, that no such adequate substitute can be provided for the present system, Parliament should, at this critical moment, unguardedly yield to the demands of the Company, and give its sanction to their claims to a *perpetuity* of those privileges which they have hitherto been contented to receive *with limitation*, what difficulties would it not entail upon its own future proceedings? If the *corporate sovereignty* of the Company is once absolutely *engrafted* upon *the Sovereignty of the State*, it cannot be extracted without lacerating the ancient stock, and convulsing the general system.

The Company would have done wisely, if, instead of resting their case upon pretensions erroneous in fact, inadmissible in law, and derogatory of the authority addressed, they had rested it wholly upon their own endeavours to promote the original purpose of their incorporation: namely, *the honour of the Crown*, and *the advantage of the commonwealth*. Upon that ground the Company might have stood strong; and all that would then have remained for the consideration of Parliament, would have been a question, how those great interests could, under existing circumstances, be best advanced; either by continuing the present arrangement without alteration, or by modifying it in such particulars, as Parliament in its wisdom might judge to be necessary. But instead of this, they have taken ground upon high pretensions of RIGHT, which must necessarily provoke investigation; and we have discovered, in the foregoing inquiry, how far those pretensions are supported.

The determination of this great question, however, is now reserved for Parliament; and, upon the wisdom of Parliament, the Country may with confidence rely, for a full consideration of all the public rights, commercial as well as political; and likewise, for the final adoption of such an arrangement for the government and trade of India, as shall appear to be the best calculated to advance the real interests, and to promote the general prosperity of the Empire, both in the East and West.

GRACCHUS.

THE END.

Printed by Libri Plureos GmbH in Hamburg,
Germany